Poetry Of The Inner Path

By Mary T. Harris

Copyright © 2007 by Mary T. Harris

This work is licensed under the Creative Commons Attribution-Noncommercial-No Derivative Works 3.0 License. The poetry in this book may be copied, distributed, displayed and presented but must not be changed. Also, the poet must be acknowledged, and the poetry may not be used for any commercial purposes.

To view a copy of this license, visit http://creativecommons.org/licenses/by-nc-nd/3.0/ or send a letter to Creative Commons, 171 Second Street, Suite 300, San Francisco, California, 94105, USA.

Published by Weber Harris Publishing
wh.publishing@gmail.com

Printed in the United States Of America

ISBN 978-0-6151-5696-5

Front cover design by Philip H. Weber

Dedication:

For all those who dare to seek light and love
in every moment

The sect of lovers is distinct from all others,
Lovers have a religion and a faith of their own.
Though the ruby has no stamp, what matters it?
Love is fearless in the midst of the sea of fear.

The Religion of Love
By Rúmí (*Translation F. Hadland Davis*)

Acknowledgements:

I gratefully acknowledge the following people:

For my loving husband, who has given me great support and encouragement in my efforts of publishing this book, thank you.

For my parents and siblings, your unconditional love, encouragement and inspiration over the years have meant so much to me, and I am eternally grateful to you.

For my friends, thank you for your support, advice and encouragement.

You are love in form.

Contents

Title	Page
Divine Light Of The Moon	1
A Miracle Everywhere	2
The Folly Of Egoic Anger	3
Intrepid Gatekeeper	4,5
The Bonds Of Love	6
In Search Of You	7
Unwavering Angel	8
My Cat, My Projection	9
Entertain The Light	10
Spirit Of The Moment	11
Sweet Seraphim	12
The Beautiful Meagerness Of Words	13
Ancient Illusions	14
The Dragon Of Obsession	15
Windows Of The Soul	16
Universe	17
Venerable, Courageous Mariner	18
Nostalgic Joy	19
Woman	20
A Moment In Heaven	21
Forever Love	22
The Peace Of Forgiveness	23
The Dragon In My Queendom	24
Always The Dawn	25
Fear Unveiled	26
Oh Divine Moment	27
Turn Toward The Glorious Nothingness	28

Contents

Title	Page
Sweet Cherries	29
Coming To The Heart	30
All Is One	31
Autumn Sunday	32
A Rose For Eternity	33
Allowing Joy	34
Sweet Freedom	35
Dancing Spirit	36
Just Be	37
The Grand Illusionist	38
The Courage To Surrender	39
Angels, Show Him The Way	40
Spirit Storm	41
To Weep, Yes To Breathe	42
Devotion To The Journey	43
Welcome Home	44
Wisdom Of The Heart	45
Mother's Eternal Love	46,47
The Non-Dualistic Self	48
To Go Beyond The Mystique	49
True Nature	50
Delicate Deliverance	51
The Lighted Path	52
Joyful Traveler	53
The Enchanting Dance Of Love	54
Lift Up	55
Beyond Self	56

Divine Light Of The Moon

The moon shines brightly tonight
Sandy craters forming a gentle
And wise face, watching
Ever faithfully from above.

I gaze in awe at the beauty
I have seen thousands of times before
A serenity rarely felt on this earth
Shares itself and I do not question.

My soul is reminded and reconnected
By these few brief moments
Lightened, renewed, comforted
I tear myself away from the sky.

One last glance, but maybe two
With the wonder of a child
I stand without words, peacefully,
Without thoughts, in blissful harmony.

A Miracle Everywhere

Magnolia leaves sprinkled so delicately
Intricate handprints of God
Decorating with intricate simplicity
Just as alive as the tree from whence you came.

Grand magnolia, sweet matriarch,
You tower over all of your friends
Protectively, in sweet nurturing
Joining with them in synchronous harmony.

Your companion, the mulberry tree,
Stands near you in mutual celebration
Sharing the same bountiful earth
Baring its pink blossoms in perfect union.

The sun shines its brilliance
On the canopies and blossoms
Sending love back to the universe
Knowing each branch and petal is the same miracle.

The Folly Of Egoic Anger

Oh sweet dagger of the heart
You are alluring and consuming,
A cunning master of illusion
Tricking the unaware into taking you in.

Your power and righteousness give
A glory in painful loneliness
A self-worth from others' validation
A fulfillment false and empty.

Your jagged edge cuts deeply
Destroying trust, violating the heart
Wreaking havoc on love itself but
Cloaked as a warrior of truth.

As you appear in your costume
Of greatness and grandeur
Let your folly be exposed and
Your dubious charms disappear forever.

Intrepid Gatekeeper

I venture into the cave again
Feeling untouchable, wearing plated armor
And I remember the one true soul
And smile as I encounter the gatekeeper.

Filled with light she greets me
Sharing enthusiasm for my adventures
And telling stories of her own
With a half-hearted smile.

Elves rush by with dark deeds
Stopping only to sniff and grunt
Before they run to finish errands
For their duchess of destruction.

I shake off their mental madness
But feel the omnipresent doom encircling me
Foul and insidious, it has permeated
The hearts and minds of many in this darkness.

Suddenly the white sorceress appears
And waves her wand at the gatekeeper
The wise keeper complies, but her eyes show
The spell of this captivator has not bewitched her.

I remember the magic queen's repertoire
Of sinister schemes and hollow words
And invite the altruistic gatekeeper
To venture out of the gloom of the cave.

She accepts but cannot see the path
A glimmer of hope staying in her deepest heart
She smiles and hugs me in gratitude
And waves me on to my next adventure.

With a quickened pace, I leave the cavern
Glad to be escaping the magic malevolence
But leaving a part of my heart with the kind
Soul who always fearlessly remained in the light.

The Bonds Of Love

I miss you more than the stars in the universe
All the waves in the oceans could never compare
The grains of sands on the earth could only hope
The fire in the sun seems only a meager flame.

You have gone into the spiritual beyond and
My heart has been broken open forever
I can only wish to see you in my dreams
And then be so blessed as to remember your visit.

No one can ever take your place, sweet mother,
You hold a place so precious within my heart and soul
That it cannot be truly touched by any human,
Any eloquent words, any beautiful melodies.

Only pure Love can touch the place in my heart
Where you reside, because you were only peace,
Only compassion, only sweetness, only serenity
You were only and all, kind spirit.

You gave me life, and then showed me
The only way to truly have life
Is to love deeply in every moment
And I could not ask for a greater gift.

And now I know in my deepest heart
That beneath my grief is my love for you,
And that you will always be with me
Because the bonds of love can never be broken…

In Search of You

If you climbed Mount Everest
Conquered the stock market
Drove a Maserati
You still wouldn't find you.

If you lived in a mansion
Wore only designer clothing
Took expensive, luxury-filled trips
You still wouldn't see you.

If you owned corporations
Held the position of executive
Earned millions every year
You still wouldn't know you.

If you were an influential politician
Traveled all over the world
Wielded power over many
You still wouldn't control you.

All of the possessions and obsessions
In the world are not the real you
Only the one who shines from beneath all of these
Worldly things waiting to be heard, is you.

Unwavering Angel

She, with her attitude and flair
Struts with independence
Bares her soul with little fear
Cares with the heart of a lion.

Her love is fierce and gentle
Demanding truth ferociously
Seeking peace tenaciously
Sharing her heart generously.

Those who dare to be with her
Risk their hearts to be torn open
Their lives purified of deception
Their spirits dancing in joy and bliss.

Each moment an exploration of what is
Her journey is a grand adventure
Allowing life to be just as it is
Stepping when the spirit moves her.

She, with her attitude and flair
Shines light wherever she goes
Inspires others to walk their paths
Shares her fierce gift endlessly.

She can be no other…

My Cat, My Projection

For My Feline Son, A Tongue-In-Cheek Story

Dear Furry Feline, I must ask, what you do know?
What do think about life and where it will go?
Do you feel happy and thusly do you feel sad?
When you get your way do you feel grateful and glad?

Some say you're a mystery but I disagree
I think you're like a human, similar to me
You love all the attention and much royal care
You're obsessive like me with your volumes of hair.

You love gourmet food and rich salmon treats
Your blanket is sheepskin, your bed I must heat
You require much hugging and kisses galore
When we give you some you always want more.

You demand that we rise at the break of the dawn
We quickly attend to you with many a yawn
You climb on our laps to luxuriate then leave
We wonder which of our habits is your pet peeve.

If you're like your mom in your personality
Then you'll like some diamonds and lots of TLC
You'll want all the luxuries that life has to share
You'll want an ease-y life, in the world not a care.

Entertain The Light

Entertain not the ifs and shoulds and thens
Alluring and exhilarating though they may be
For only may they be the brain's prattle
To keep itself busy and think itself wise.

Entertain not the should haves and would haves
For they are close cousins of guilt and guile
And never have breathed the fresh spring air
Nor seen the bright light of day.

Entertain not the whens and thens
For too closely a friendship will fashion
The present into a misery of waiting
Rather than a joy and aliveness in living.

Rather, let the present entertain you, if you dare
The sway of daffodils dancing in the wind
The freshness of a mindful moment
The precious smile of a loved one.

For where can life display its innate magnificence
Its constant stream of miracles and truths
The beauty and compassion that can only be felt
With the heart, if not here and now?

Let the present envelop you in its spacious eternity
Where judgment flees in the presence of truth
Where joy is alive in the moment
And the spirit dances in celebration…

Spirit Of The Moment

A sweet melody graces my ears
And my heart begins to sing
Shivers roll down my spine
In perfect harmony with the wind.

A simple song of few notes
Its peace and serenity
Calms and comforts
The roaring beast within.

A pungent, delicious aroma
Wafts through the air, enticing
Owning my appetite and desire
Bringing precious memories of loved ones.

Children play with abandon
Bravely challenging life
To be all that it will be
Accepting each moment just as it is.

I savor the perfection of imperfection
Cherishing this existence and its one clear truth
Allowing the spirit to permeate every moment
Presenting my life among all others in a delightful dance…

Sweet Seraphim

Ethereal sentinel, filled with light and love
Your face must be beautiful beyond earthly brilliance
You bring Divine purpose in all of your biddings
You are a messenger with miracles in devoted humility.

I feel your presence day and night
Calling on you in desperation, joy and sorrow
You are happy to bring heavenly peace and love
Helping to open my eyes to the truth within.

Dearest protector, you steer me away from
Harm and suffering in your mysterious ways
And inspire the wisdom to listen quietly
To your protective advice and counsel.

My heart leaps and dances with joy
Knowing you are always by my side
Guiding me along my destined path
Reminding me of my perfect free will.

Sweet angel, gentle keeper of my life
My heart and soul I share with you humbly
In deep gratitude for your loving service
I will cherish you every moment, forever…

The Beautiful Meagerness Of Words

Though one may say virtuous words
Though they may bathe the heart in light
Connecting others in a transcending love
The words can only be pointers to the truth.

Though one may love words and their meanings
Expressing them in a certain, unique way
Reflecting the wonder and beauty of this life
They can only touch the profoundness of this existence.

Though one may connect with loved ones in words
Allowing one to bridge the distance of personalities
Creating and nurturing wondrous relationships
Words can barely express the depth of love.

Though one may entertain oneself with words
Engage one's mind in intellectual curiosities
Filling it with useful facts and interesting trivia
Words can only touch upon the Divine design of this life.

Though words may bring great acclaim and success
Inspire grand literary works and heart-filled songs
Bringing great joy and meaning to others
They can only touch upon what the spirit already knows.

Ancient Illusions

Rich in the treasures of the heart
You are abundant in the spirit's beauty
Alone and protected behind safe walls
You are truly seen by precious few.

Jagged words and deeds have pierced deeply
And plentifully, the heart marred unconsciously,
Your trust in the world has given way
To a master of illusion and fear.

Your stone walls fortified and unyielding
Shielding boldly from attack
Also serve as a cold, jagged barrier
To the warmth of love and life.

Kind words barely penetrating these ancient lies,
There you lie in suffering, never allowing
Another to truly enter your precious domain
Your light muted and diffuse to all but you.

The Dragon Of Obsession

Dear heart, so charming and alluring
With eyes engaging and smile provocative
Entrancing many hearts with few words
Leaving them blindly spinning, ever hopeful.

The adoration, obsequious and naïve,
A golden vision of majesty and grandeur
Serves a false god with imagined exaltation
Belying an unattended emptiness within.

The heart may not be seen nor felt
Though it may ask many times
The wisdom may not be discovered
Though the soul may yearn endlessly.

To deny the truth, one will not see
The dragon of obsession lives among the clouds
Throwing down bolts of fiery lightening
Serving only itself, mocking humanity wickedly.

Windows Of The Soul

Engaging with the eyes,
Fair heart and curious mind
May not turn away in denial
Discounting the beauty of the rose.

Engaging with the eyes,
Dark clouds and bright moons
Cannot be dismissed into nothingness
For the heart can never forget.

Engaging with the eyes,
The mind craftily convinces
Nothing can inflict harm but
Later discovers the soul emblazoned.

Engaging with the eyes,
The soul is touched every moment
But the wise need only feed it
With eternal and abundant sustenance.

Universe

In you there is a universe
Expansive, ever-changing
Allowing of the tides
Living free in the moment.

The vastness that is you
Can only be touched upon
With mere words and ideas
Such is the beauty of this life.

Your heart is led peacefully
In the pursuit of truth
And dances in delight
Seeing the true spirit in others.

You cannot be trifled
With fear or anxiety
Knowing there is nothing
To be frightened of, nothing to hide.

You are love and peace in form
A deep celebration of life
A manifestation of Divinity
The universe alive in beauty…

Venerable, Courageous Mariner

Grand matriarch, proud and intrepid
You are a beautiful ship
That has sailed many seas
And ventured to many exotic lands.

Though wind and rain have tattered
Your mast many times and
Rust has dared to invade your hull,
Your voyage continues undaunted.

Though hurricanes and icebergs
Have thrashed your bow and stern
And barnacles have burdened your shell
Your spirit is rebuilt and renewed tenaciously.

You have sailed to unknown territories
Charted new routes with an unyielding compass
Conquered the fiercest of obstacles
In your unending quest for life and liberty.

Magnificent vessel of the high seas
Neither storm nor encumbrance can dissuade you
So let out your jib and pull in your anchor
You were always meant to sail into the sunlight…

Nostalgic Joy

Radiant pinks stream softly
Peaches and purples streak gently
Painting the sunset with tender strokes
Reminiscent of sweet and simple times

Of handmade dresses and hand-me-downs
Picking fragrant flowers for Mom
And the beloved teacher at school
Of finger painting playfully with abandon

Dressing dolls up in fabric pieces and string
Playing hopscotch on chalky sidewalks
Hide-n-go-seek with friends outside until dark
Feeling the chill of the evening on my skin

Running through the sprinkler in summer
Crunching through the leaves in autumn
Splashing through the rain in winter
Flying kites and riding bikes in spring

Living in the moment, allowing it to be
Velvety streams and streaks waft gently through
Lingering, smiling and dancing
Celebrating with abandon the joyful child within…

Woman

As I look in the mirror into my own eyes
A different face appears in the silvery looking glass,
And I am drawn to gaze further at
The stranger who is peering back at me,
Curious for someone who looks everyday.

Beyond all of the unrest and defenses,
Beyond all of the expectations of others,
Peace and serenity live undisturbed
Acceptance and forgiveness live undaunted,
Sweetness and wisdom live untainted.

Failures in life fade in the face of truth
Shining so omnipotently and somehow
Blend into the perfect circle of one,
Each piece a part of the puzzle,
Each bend and twist a part of the journey.

In a sacred moment, quietly, peacefully, gently
The beauty that can only come from beyond,
The knowing of many generations before me
Give their blessing to my life and I humbly
Kneel in peace and wonder.

A Moment In Heaven

I walked in the sunlit forest with my love
Into a dream although awake
Nature displaying its glory fantastically
As if only created for our delight.

A fawn greeted us shyly, inviting a magical
Journey, then disappeared like a kindly elf
Venturing on we discovered towering canopies,
A mystical coolness and verdant fields of ferns.

Gentle streams with mini-waterfalls graced our path
Before we found the sun splashing generously
Our steps lined with lilies, poppies and buttercups
Before us a view of majestic, green mountains.

Next in the dream, a picturesque little pond
Filled with tall, green reeds and ducks hiding
Spying on each other, chasing and splashing,
Skinks and quail sunning themselves happily.

Further on peacocks proudly displayed
Iridescent green and blue plumage, singing their
Wild, melodic calls to delight their peahens
Inviting us to reconnect in the circle of life.

A fairy tale beyond any dream
We traced our path back in wonder and awe
Just beating the sun in its colorful farewell
Only to see the same fawn, extending another invitation…

Forever Love

For My Husband

Did you come to me in my dreams
In the soft, sweet flow of consciousness
Between wake and sleep
Where cherubs must certainly reside?

Did we meet in an adventure
Otherworldly and fantastic
Climbing Mount Everest in a day
Flying in a hot air balloon among the clouds?

Did you speak my name with 1000 angels
Promising God your unending devotion to me
Calling on the sun to brighten our days and
The moon to bring a celestial glow to our nights?

Did you ask the universe to send roses and lilacs
Butterflies and bluebirds, lions and lemurs
Life in all of its wondrous mystery
To delight our senses and inspire our souls?

Everything you touch is permeated with love
Every breath you exhale infuses the world with love
And every heart around you is filled generously,
Joyfully, and gently with love, my dear.

The Peace Of Forgiveness

The stars shine brightly as
I breathe in the night air
Feeling the pull of the unseen
Being led to places unknown.

The fire jumps and dances
Celebrating life's mystery as
A quiet void appears, inviting me
To relax into its peace and harmony.

People who have wronged me appear
And I see that they were victims
Of their insecurities and fears,
Missing the love of the Divine.

Forgiveness begins knowing they were estranged
From themselves, from their Divine purpose,
Un-conscious of their actions and words,
Only faintly hearing the call of their spirits.

The Dragon In My Queendom

Again I jump as the dragon spews his flames
My heart pounding and my pulse racing
I act quickly with survival instinct to fend
Off the beast that will certainly bring harm.

He looks at me snarling and baring his teeth
Wanting only to destroy me in his fire
And I draw my sword and lunge forward
Hoping the monster will retreat to his lair.

The dragon laughs uproariously as I fight
Courageously to end his evil rampage
Then swings his sharp-edged tail towards me
Sending me flying into a crevasse jagged and deep.

I climb out with determination
Ready to do battle again with the demon
And run behind him for a surprise attack when
He turns around suddenly, ready to destroy me.

Bravely I yell, stay then dragon!
You will not hurt me or annihilate me!
And before my eyes, the dragon magically
Disappears leaving a mound of precious gems.

Always The Dawn

To see the past in his eyes
And yet, to look again
To see future's dreams
Never darkness, but always the dawn.

There is hope and inspiration
Amid the burning embers
Of the past and the raging
Fire of the future.

I can sense his journey
When his eyes show unhappiness
A past to learn and feel
A future to become and live.

Leading him on to seek
Like the unceasing waves of the ocean
He follows and searches
But there is always the dawn.

I see eternity in his eyes...

Fear Unveiled

Spinning, spiraling into an abyss
The questions become more intense
Biting away at the core of beliefs
Leaving nothing but a wind blustering through.

Panic and fear dance about in folly
Reminding of concerns and duties
Reprimanding like a stern parent
Knowing they are of little essence.

The unruly storm subsides in misery
Realizing the fun is tragically over
In the midst of a greater force
Bringing truth beyond worldly wisdom.

The calm begins to take root tenaciously
Digging up fallacies of long ago
Dissolving them into forgiving memories
Leaving a garden of truth to cherish...

Oh Divine Moment

The moment is forever
But to join this eternity
Mysteriously outside of time
Grace in its wisdom may only bestow.

You beckon peacefully
Filled with joy and wisdom
Beyond worldly wisdom
For you know the truth, you are life.

For the true and courageous
You graciously impart
Freshness of heart and knowing of spirit
A gift of love beyond all others.

But you cannot speak nor be heard clearly
If worldly sounds hinder your voice
If worldly concerns misconstrue your message
If worldly pace thwarts your purpose.

Only in the quietness of the heart
With slow, loving intention
A deep breath bringing life
May you speak clearly, eternally.

Turn Toward The Glorious Nothingness

In this grand adventure, will you succumb
To the temptation of fighting monsters,
Wielding swords and maces
Only seeking to conquer and win?

Will you stand on the highest pedestal
Watching the lowly muddle about
Cursing the darkness angrily
Never offering to share your light?

Can you fill your precious moments
With the sound of emptiness
The chatter of unconsciousness
Hungry ghosts constantly feasting?

Can you turn away from the sun,
The sky, the stars, the trees
The beauty offered munificently
For a barren treasure chest in a distant cave?

Can you turn away from the true adventure
The voyage in the deepest ocean
The exploration that yields no gold,
But brings abundance beyond measure?

Sweet Cherries

Sweet cherries generously kissed by the sun
Nurtured by watchful rain and wind
Blessed be the vines that gave birth
To your precious, sweet essence.

Your blossoms, little bursts of heaven,
Fill the air with a gentle fragrance
Your petals floating magically on the wind
Cascading peacefully into a pink paradise.

Sweet cherries, brilliant and shining
May your sweetness never be turned
By the harshness of flood and drought
And you always reach for the sun to find your way…

Coming To The Heart

Quicken the pace said the Rabbit nervously
For there are things to do and people to see
I shudder to think we won't finish our work
Our bosses will think our duties we will shirk.

No, said the Tortoise, we can't do it that way
We should take our own time and enjoy our day
If we do some tasks well, I'm sure we'll be fine
Our bosses will like us, we'll certainly shine.

Oh no, said the Rabbit more insistently
That way is slow and some tasks won't be complete
We'll fall behind in life and get in trouble
We'll earn only half instead of making double.

The Tortoise looked over and smiled pleasantly
Well it all depends on who you want to be
Life will reward you when you come from your heart
You'll have love and prosperity doing your part.

But what does that mean? asked Rabbit anxiously
How will I finish my work and feel happy?
I run and I run, I work myself crazy
Just so the others won't think I am lazy.

Well look at it this way said Tortoise gently
Your life so precious can be lived mindfully
To your deepest heart you must always be true
To live from faith, not fear, is what you can do.

I see said Rabbit as he smiled happily
Living in the moment is where I will be
Choosing love above all in life's mystery
I'll work and play embracing peace mindfully.

All Is One

My Love,
Can the sun be more glorious than the moon?
Can the stars be more wondrous than the planets?
Does the daffodil envy the rose's beauty?
Does the ladybug ever wish to be a butterfly?

How can magnificence outshine magnificence?
Silly comparison only comes forth
In the moment when the mind
Tries in vain to be omnipotent.

The ocean meets the thirsty earth
And rejoices in their union.
The rivers dance in celebration
As they fill with spring's bounty.

The sky welcomes the clouds warmly
Inviting them to share her paradise
As the two paint the horizon
In Divine, colorful play.

My Love, no heart can love life
More than another in truth
No destiny can be more precious
Than another for those who love.

Autumn Sunday

For Mom and Dad

The sun streaming in on a lazy day
Quiet rumblings of children at play
Leaves rustling around enjoying the wind
Birds singing softly, the soul at mend.

Nature displaying glorious sites and scents
Letting us be just in the moment
Peacefully we put the noisy mind to rest
Seeing all with which we have been blessed.

A time to withdraw, a time to slow down
The signs of calming are all around
The sun gracing us with shorter days
Mother Nature is showing us the way.

Soon the coolness will nip the face
Over the land the leaves will lace
Rain and snow will come for a time
Precious serenity for the soul to find.

A Rose For Eternity

Small, protected, and nurtured
The rosebud is born on the vine
Allowing the sun to brings its glory
Welcoming the blessings of the rain.

Neither darkness not scarcity
Threatens its beauty and truth
The rose flourishes each day
Sharing its joy and brilliance.

The blossom spreads its petals
As the universe celebrates blissfully
In the fullness of its beauty
Knowing it can never be diminished.

Kindly the days come when the petals
Lose some of their luster and shine
But the rose can not weep or mourn for
The journey will always be blessed.

Eventually the glorious blossom finishes
Its wondrous and bountiful journey
Dropping from the grateful vine
Peacefully bidding farewell, never truly departed...

Allowing Joy

A sleepy day begins
As I nurture a grateful heart
The sun peeks in through the curtains
Inviting a wondrous and adventurous day.

Driving into work
The trees are greeting the day
Blossoming in rich glory
Sharing their Divine beauty with all.

The clouds are gracing the sky
The two in vibrant conversation
Old friends spending cherished time
Creating miracles in the simplicity of being.

As the day of duties begins
Each one presents itself freely
An activity to stir energy and creativity
The universe kindly giving challenge and reward.

Coworkers talking, laughing
Sharing stories of spouses, children, travel
Knowing deeply in their hearts
They are truly sharing love.

The ride home brings a kind goodbye
Of tired and grateful workers
All pushing homeward to families
Anticipation shining through on every face.

A wondrous and beautiful adventure
Each day can be no less
For every moment offers a miracle
For the heart that truly wants to see.

Sweet Freedom

Gentle breeze blowing
Through my mind
Where do you come from
Sweet purveyor of clarity?

Your grand wisdom cannot come
From the roaring machinery
That dominates each moment
Mercilessly with an iron fist.

Your sense of deep connection cannot
Be taken from the linear logic
Of ten million firing neurons
Frantically looking for life's answers.

Your profound peace cannot come
From the mind's chaos and noise
That interweaves each moment
With anxiety and unrest.

Gentle breeze, sweet truth
My mind would dare to touch
But could never hope to grasp
And steps aside in peaceful obeisance.

Dancing Spirit

The beauty and spaciousness of a clear, blue sky
The sun shining on the ocean creating an endless glitter
The infinite number of stars twinkling for many generations
Only may I truly see if I awaken to my truth.

The connection and depth of understanding of a close friend
The warmth of the heart when you help someone in need
The unconditional love and acceptance of your soul mate
Only may I feel if I truly open my heart and allow vulnerability.

The sound of children playing and laughing
The total enjoyment of listening to your favorite songs
The warmth and security of hearing your soul mate's voice
Only may I truly hear when I am quietly listening.

The perfume of honeysuckle on a warm spring day
The fresh scent of a baby's skin
The rustic fragrance of the forest after a rain
Only may I inhale wondrous beauty if I stop to savor the moment.

The warmth of a long-needed hug
The sweetness of a kiss from a loved one
The simple pleasure of holding hands, walking on the beach
Only may I truly live in joy if I awaken my spirit and let it dance
every moment...

Just Be

If you could not make the wind blow
Or compel it to stop in its fury
Honoring its flow and purpose,
The wind would naturally go on its way.

If you could not create the tides
Or calm them in their ferocity
In the magnificence of the universe,
The tides would flow in their cycle of life.

If you could not make the sun shine
Or cool it when it ravaged the earth,
In its mysterious, life-giving way,
The sun would shine and hide in perfection.

If you could not create the essence of life
The basic elements of love and peace
The purity of beauty and joy
You would simply just be...

And life would flow infinitely through you...

The Grand Illusionist

Oh clever chameleon, you are artful in the enslavement of souls, disguising yourself in ornate designs of gold and silver, convincing the unsuspecting of your false omnipotence, all the while stealing their hearts, their humanity, their innate knowing.

The susceptible exalt you above all else, buying into your lies, until they come to believe that your biddings make them special, superior. In your insidious and deceptive ways, you have convinced them, malicious marauder, that you will rescue them out of their lowly humanity, and make them superhuman, with all of your empty finery.

Until life turns the tide of you, the unsuspecting see the true miracle and see you as you truly are, a fraud, and that you have duped them into believing in destructive illusions.

Then your house of cards will fall, false friend, your true color of darkness will show, and the world will finally see you as you truly are: an insidious lie that humanity and the earth can no longer believe in nor tolerate.

The Courage To Surrender

Shall I sail on the ocean
The turquoise waters that promise
Nothing to wind and sky
The vast openness that answers to no one?

Shall I succumb to its peace
And yet to its turbidity
Its gentleness and waves of chaos
The sea of wisdom that makes sense of all?

Will I let it engulf my heart
My mind, my spirit
Bringing me on an daring adventure
Giving me a home that compares to none?

Will the mysterious ocean
Grace me with its light
Share with me its love
And bless me with its serenity?

Will I muster my courage
And open my clouded eyes
To see that the grand voyage has
Already entranced my soul and set sail?

Angels, Show Him The Way

For M.H., Rest In Peace And Joy

In a flash of angry fire
Gone was his life and his love
Sad and heartbroken, we could
Only find solace from above.

Memories flooding in
Guilt and theories too
Our minds could not accept
What our hearts already knew.

The soul felt torn to shreds
The human grief so deep
No one could understand
But prayed God his soul to keep.

His life was precious and dear
His heart was giving and kind
A sweet legacy of love
We were all so blessed to find.

He said his earthly farewell
In sweetness and bliss he'll be
We wish him love and peace
In a life so heavenly.

Spirit Storm

The winds blew hard sometimes
They came with no warning
Whirlwinds of great intensity
Picking up everything in their path.

The roofs gave way first
Leaving little protection from the fury
Everything inside thrown around mercilessly
Pieces of life's necessities strewn all throughout.

Suddenly the house came off its foundation
Spinning through the air wildly
Finally landing in a foreign place
While the storm calmed mysteriously.

But the walls humbly fell, the floors gave way
The remains of a decrepit building submitting
And just a few steps away, a palace awaited
Offering peace, serenity, gentle winds…

To Weep, Yes To Breathe

Your tears flow like a stream
Made of drops of pure gold
Each one precious and dear
Opening the doors of the heart
Allowing the spirit to breathe life
Like raindrops making way for the sun.

Your shining tears, they cast no shame
No weakness can these precious drops bear
For they are great treasures pouring from within
A courageous vulnerability borne of spirit
Stripped of all ideas and conceptions
The true essence of humanness,
The true heart, a precious gift from God…

Devotion To The Journey

To love truly
A fraction can not know
A drop compared to infinity
Judgment can never bestow.

To touch the light
Working hands may persuade
But without heartful intent
They can only sweetly aid.

To see the truth
Spirit can only avail
Mere thoughts can only admire
For Love will always prevail.

Welcome Home

For My Father

Step through the gentle portal
Of light and love, faithful servant
Where angels and friends await
With unending joy and celebration.

Cast your coat of angst aside
For words unspoken, deeds undone
For I alone know your heart and I
Know your deepest motivation was love.

Carry no fear for what will be
For we have built a castle
For you and your loved ones and
Heaven will bless you infinitely in its glory.

Be not sad for the ones
You have temporarily parted with
For your bond of love is eternal
And you can never truly be separated.

Welcome home good and faithful servant
You have loved me with your whole heart
You have shared me in your loving service and
I await your arrival to hold you gently in my arms.

Wisdom of the Heart

I sit amused wondering how the thief got away
So quickly and stole such precious gems
She took what was so long my ultimate
Pride and joy, my power and confidence,
My "secret" weapon in the world.
Shining eyes reaching out to share,
Skin so youthful, a body voluptuous,
Somehow I felt these jewels would never fade.
But the eyes finding wrinkles deeper with time,
The tummy finding itself more soft and round,
I could obsess and lament the changes of time
But instead I smile and welcome Lady Nature
Yes, come and bring your richness and color.
My eyes that have smiled, danced and frowned,
My arms and legs that have worked and played,
My body that has shared love and life,
I can only be grateful for these gifts
That life has so generously brought to me,
And I laugh at the thief amused and delighted…

Mother's Eternal Love

For My Mother

It rains again softly
And I think of her
Holding her picture
As I often do.

She looks back at me
Her smile genuine
Her eyes shining
And I feel love eternal.

More raindrops fall gently
And the winds begin to blow
Sweet memories waft through
And I wish she were here.

But then I step back and feel
Truth envelop my heart
And Life shows its mystery of
Perfection in a design of imperfection.

Her life was love and human frailty,
Devotion and distance,
And my heart understands that somehow
This was perfectly Divine.

Her spirit was freed from this
Physical existence, but never gone
For she could never truly
Be separated from her loved ones.

Peacefully the rains subside
Realizing their season is over
And the winds wondrously
Calm to a delicate peace…

The Non-Dualistic Self

Within the intricate layers beneath

Live the simple truths

Of emotions beautiful and thoughts complex

Of the heart passionate and soul serene

Of the past romanticized and present alive

Of humanness egoic and spiritualness Divine

All connected, all one.

Love stands guard powerfully and gently

Protecting the treasures given by One

Shared perfectly and heartfully with many

Pilfered nor taken by none, resting eternally.

To Go Beyond The Mystique

The past, as a wily fox,
So too a taskmaster,
Gives only sweet fruit
As the sun shines benevolently.

The mind, in concert too,
No hearth or home
Can not bear the majestic beauty
Only trained repetitions and entreaties.

Blind shackles hold prisoner
The heart that will not forgive
Love searching but not finding
Until the surrender is sweeter than the mystique.

True Nature

So the river flows gently over the rocks
In luminous sheets, glistening and
Sparkling in peaceful exuberance
Never knowing where it may traverse.

Junipers and pines blissfully
Wave and sway in friendship
The bluebirds happily bathe
In a quiet oasis near the shore.

Foxes and deer eagerly come
Bobcats and lions too
Gratefully imbibing in the glistening drops
Always thirsting to drink from the source.

The earth tenderly holds the flow
Giving where it may need
Changing with the wisdom of the tide
In sweet union and synchronicity.

Joyfully the sun shines
Warming the river on its way
Bringing light to its wondrous journey
Lovingly illuminating its intrinsic beauty.

Delicate Deliverance

I hide away in a quiet world
Admiring the oak tree swaying in the wind,
Watching the daffodils and marigolds
In their merry, sweet dance.

Allowing the simple joys to nourish me
In a peaceful and protective cocoon
I am shielded from life's jagged edges
Living delicately from moment to moment.

The scent of the rose lingers
Only wanting to sooth my tattered soul
The sun shines its light compassionately
Only seeking to lift my bedraggled mind.

So I take careful steps
Bending and swaying with the oak tree
Allowing Love to continue its bountiful blessings
Knowing deliverance comes gently in the moment…

The Lighted Path

Love, I am yours always
I could never be otherwise
I walk in you, breathe in you
Immerse myself in you completely.

Where I may feel lack
I drink from you with abandon
And pour you bountifully,
Truthfully and humbly.

Where I may feel abundance
I celebrate your goodness
Sharing with all who may receive
And thank you with a grateful heart.

I enjoin you, submit to you,
Exalt you, peacefully reside in you
Every moment is your miracle
Every miracle is your benevolent gift.

Joyful Traveler

In the flowing, whispery winds
You are there touching the soul
In the luxuriant, radiant blossom
You are there delighting the heart.

The mountains call longingly
The trees welcome warmly
The animals befriend in love
The skies reflect in glory.

The Divine oneness of life
All around, in the moment
Calling, reminding, inspiring
Beautifying the darkest moments.

And yet one moment stands
Enraptured and unbelieving
Another moment crawls and
Creeps hindered and comical.

The head and the heart duel
And finally delight in making peace
Knowing in the end that life is a
Display for the watchful traveler

A mysterious dream beyond all others…

The Enchanting Dance Of Love

Oh Love, how you dance so joyfully
And sing sweet melodies
And play in the garden of our hearts.

How you shine so brilliantly
And bring your wondrous gifts in
Joining two spirits as one.

How can we ever know your
Mysterious ways dear Love
In your beautiful dance from blossom to blossom?

Only may we celebrate your delightful expression
Sharing our unending joy with Heaven
Bidding the angels to tend ever sweetly, ever gently.

Lift Up

Worries do not trifle
For your vehemence is false
Your repertoire is unnecessary
Your sword is dull and
Your story is illusive
So I say again, do not trifle.

You cannot know the true joy
In the daily flow of miracles
For all you truly know is the
Empty contentment of your lies,
The sweet panic when one no
Longer chooses to entertain you.

So I cast you into the heavens
Your unconscious, undeserved power
Your chaos and empty thrills
Your useless acting and bravado
And gently my hand is taken,
Quietly my soul is lifted.

Beyond Self

Let me go in the mist of your cold fog
Where mystery cloaks the truth
In powdery, dramatic confusion.

Let me go in the brightness of your sunshine
Where joy and light dance eagerly
In the sweetness and ease of life.

Let me go in the bounty of your raindrops
Where gifts are given so freely
In the generous flow of the vast tide.

Let me go in the loud thunder of your storms
Where trials test the strongest faith
In the wisdom and plan of the Divine.

Let me go in the moment of everyday
Where truth and gratitude permeate all
And I am a devoted servant to love only.

About The Poet

Mary T. Harris has written poetry for over 20 years and enjoys creating poems that reflect the wonder and awe that can be found in each moment. In addition to poetry, she also enjoys writing short stories, children's stories and song lyrics. Mary graduated from Santa Clara University with a B.S. in Anthropology and later from San Jose State University with a California multiple subject teaching credential. She currently lives with her husband in Northern California.

www.ingramcontent.com/pod-product-compliance
Lightning Source LLC
Chambersburg PA
CBHW032214040426
42449CB00005B/585